Text copyright © 2019 J. Patrick Lewis · Illustrations copyright © 2019 Miriam Nerlove
Designed by Rita Marshall; edited by Kate Riggs and Amy Novesky · Published in 2019 by Creative Editions
P.O. Box 227, Mankato, MN 56002 USA · Creative Editions is an imprint of The Creative Company
www.thecreativecompany.us · All rights reserved. No part of the contents of this book may be
reproduced by any means without the written permission of the publisher. Printed in China
Library of Congress Cataloging-in-Publication Data
Names: Lewis, J. Patrick, author. / Nerlove, Miriam, illustrator.
Title: I am polar bear / by J. Patrick Lewis; illustrated by Miriam Nerlove.
Summary: Known by many names in many languages, the polar bear remains
one of the Arctic's signature species, and as this poem reminds readers, it is "far out
on disappearing sea ice, losing hold" in a world affected by climate change.
Identifiers: LCCN 2018054982 / ISBN 978-1-56846-332-2
Subjects: LCSH: Polar bear—Arctic regions—Poetry. / Polar bear—
Effect of global warming on—Arctic regions—Poetry.
Classification: LCC PS3562.E9465 I26 2019   DDC 811/.54—dc23
First edition 9 8 7 6 5 4 3 2 1

I Am
Polar Bear

J. Patrick Lewis

illustrated by Miriam Nerlove

Creative Editions

I am Polar Bear.

Mother of Beauty,

Sister of Courage,

Fount of

Fierceness,

Heart of an All-White World,

one who calls out the poet

in all humans.

To Russians,

I am *belii medved*,

or *White Bear*,

to Danes, *isbjørn*,

or *Ice Bear*,

for many more,

simply *Sea Bear*.

Among the Inuit, I am *Nanuk*,

the animal deserving

of great respect,

or *Pihoqahiak*,

the Ever-wandering One.

The Eastern
Greenlanders
know me as
Tornassuk,
the Master of
Helping Spirits.

Norsemen, who
wear imagination
like a garment,
hail me

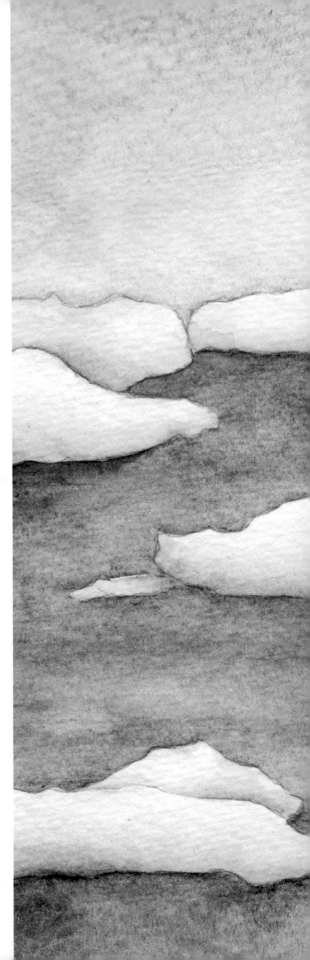

Sailor of

the Icebergs,

White Sea Deer,

Whale's Curse,

Seal's Dread.

Norse poets say
I have the strength of
twelve men and the
wits of eleven.

Siberia's Ket people
esteem all bears.
To them I am *gyp*, or
Grandfather.

The Sami people
refuse to speak
my name for fear
of offending me.
Instead, they point
to me and say,

God's Dog

or *Old Man in the Fur Coat.*

So intelligent,
those Sami.

Remember all my
names—or one.
I am Polar Bear,
the specter
far out on
disappearing
sea ice,
losing hold.

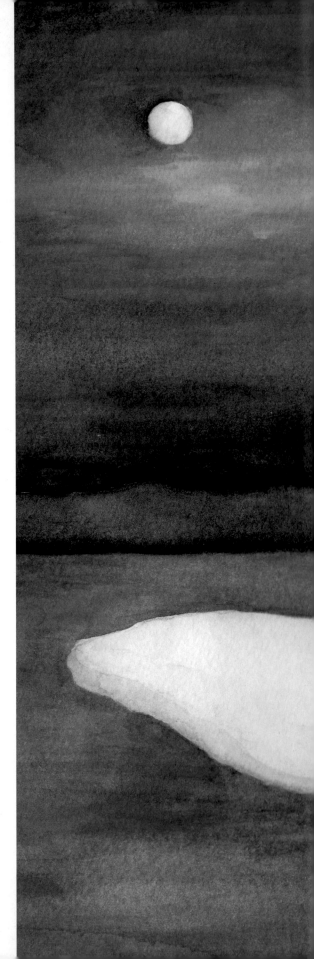

Ursus maritimus (sea bear) **Arctic habitat**: Alaska, Canada,
Russia, Greenland, and Norwegian islands **Population**: decreasing

Polar bears are majestic mammals. Males can grow to nine feet (2.7 m) in
length and weigh more than 1,500 pounds (680 kg). Polar bears live for 25 to
30 years. But how do they survive the punishing Arctic cold? A thick coat of
insulated fur covers a thick layer of fat. Under the white fur, their black skin
soaks in the sun's rays to stay warm.

These northern giants rule over their frozen domains in Alaska, Canada,
Russia, Greenland, and islands owned by Norway. They have no natural
enemies. Still, most scientists agree: The polar bear is in trouble.

The International Union for Conservation of Nature (IUCN) estimates that
there are now only about 26,000 polar bears in the wild. Yet the decreasing
availability of sea ice because of climate change limits the bears' access to
their favorite food—seals. With less ice, there are fewer seals; with fewer seals,
fewer polar bears. That is why the IUCN has listed these beautiful creatures as
"Vulnerable," and the Endangered Species Act has labeled them "Threatened."